Enlightened Risk Taking:
The Workbook

By George L. Head, Ph.D.

Copyright © 2002
by the Nonprofit Risk Management Center

ISBN No. 1-893210-10-3

**Nonprofit
Risk Management
Center**

Nonprofit Risk Management Center

The Nonprofit Risk Management Center is dedicated to helping community-serving nonprofits conserve assets, prevent harm, and free up resources for mission-critical activities. The Center provides technical assistance on risk management, liability, and insurance matters; publishes easy-to-use written resources; designs and delivers workshops and conferences; and offers competitively priced consulting services.

The Center is an independent nonprofit organization that doesn't sell insurance or endorse specific insurance providers. For more information on the products and services available from the Center, call (202) 785-3891, or visit our Web site at **www.nonprofitrisk.org**.

Nonprofit Risk Management Center
1001 Connecticut Avenue, NW
Suite 410
Washington, DC 20036
(202) 785-3891
Fax (202) 296-0349
www.nonprofitrisk.org

Staff

Sheryl Augustine, *Customer Service Representative*
Amy Michelle DeBaets, *Director of Management Information Systems*
George L. Head, Ph.D., *Special Advisor*
Suzanne M. Hensell, *Director of Marketing and Education*
Melanie L. Herman, *Executive Director*
Barbara B. Oliver, *Director of Communications*
John C. Patterson, *Senior Program Director*

Public Entity Risk Institute

The Nonprofit Risk Management Center is grateful for the support of the Public Entity Risk Institute (PERI), which provided a generous grant to support the cost of publishing this book. PERI is a tax-exempt nonprofit whose mission is to serve public, private and nonprofit organizations as a dynamic, forward thinking resource for the practical enhancement of risk management. For more information on PERI, visit the organization's Web site: **www.riskinstitute.org**.

Cover photo: © Herrmann/Starke

Table of Contents

Introduction

The Workbook, when used with *Enlightened Risk Taking: A Guide to Strategic Risk Management for Nonprofits*, is a toolkit to help managers put together a basic strategic risk management plan for a nonprofit organization. The Center invites you to work through the suggested decision processes and use the worksheets. If you record explanations and questions in *The Workbook*, The Center believes you will have a preliminary, strategic risk management plan for your nonprofit. You should then review and revise this first strategic risk management plan at least annually.

The Workbook assumes you have read all of *Enlightened Risk Taking: A Guide to Strategic Risk Management for Nonprofits* — it neither repeats the substance of that book nor leads you through it page by page. Instead, *The Workbook* presents a series of worksheets and supporting questions to guide you and your colleagues through the strategic risk management process so that, together, you can be enlightened risk takers for your nonprofit. Your focus is not on avoiding all risks — first, because risk is unavoidable in a changing world; and, second, because fulfilling the mission of any community-serving nonprofit organization requires taking risks in order to improve the world as that mission envisions. Instead, your focus is on consciously, intelligently, and responsibly taking selected risks in order to reduce potential losses and increase potential gains. Doing so should enhance the resources your nonprofit can devote to mission-critical activities. Enhancing a nonprofit's resources — protecting them from loss, expanding them where prudently possible, and stabilizing their productive use in the face of unforeseen fluctuations — is part of the fiduciary duties of trusteeship that the law imposes on a nonprofit and its leaders. Strategic risk management helps enhance these resources and fulfill these fiduciary duties.

The Table of Contents lists the titles of the worksheets in *The Workbook*, giving you an overview of your journey through strategic risk management. The sequence of the worksheets parallels the five steps in the strategic risk management process:

1. Establish the risk management context.

2. Appraise downside and upside risks — identify and prioritize them.

3. Decide what to do about these risks.

4. Act on these decisions.

5. Follow up and adjust these decisions.

The worksheets cannot perform the strategic risk management process for you. These worksheets can assist you only if you really work with them, bringing to them your special knowledge of how *your* nonprofit actually does — and ideally should — perform in an uncertain world.

In short, while it is a guide to better decision making about risk, *The Workbook* cannot be a *cookbook* that makes those decisions for you. A cookbook tells you what ingredients to use and how to process them to prepare a given result. For strategic risk management, *The Workbook* does indeed deal with process, but most of the ingredients for good decisions can only come from you and your nonprofit. There is no one universal *recipe* for sound strategic risk management decisions.

Nonetheless, just as *The Workbook* guides you through a structured risk management decision process, the staff of the Nonprofit Risk Management Center is ready to work with you in applying this process to your nonprofit. Please contact the Center if you have any questions about guiding your nonprofit along the road this journey takes or any suggestions for making the journey more rewarding. Keep in mind that the Center offers training programs throughout the year that teach the principles of strategic risk management. In addition, the Center designs and delivers customized training programs that address the specific needs of nonprofit groups. The ways to reach the Nonprofit Risk Management Center appear on the back cover of *The Workbook*.

Begin your journey through strategic risk management to a more secure, more productive future for your nonprofit. Bon Voyage!

A cookbook tells you what ingredients to use and how to process them to prepare a given result. For strategic risk management, *The Workbook* does indeed deal with process, but most of the ingredients for good decisions can only come from you and your nonprofit. There is no one universal *recipe* for sound strategic risk management decisions.

WORKSHEET 1.1   What Risk Means to You

The book *Enlightened Risk Taking* defines the word *risk* as *a measure of the possibility that the future may be surprisingly different from what we expect.* Bearing this definition in mind, consider what *risk* and its related terms — *expectations* and *uncertainty* — mean in the context of your nonprofit's daily operations. Start by seeing if you agree with some key points that are stated or implied in *Enlightened Risk Taking.*

Do You Agree?

1. Risk is a possibility, not a certainty.   ❑ Yes   ❑ No

Comments: _____

_____

2. Most people think of *risk* as only a bad thing, applying just to threats of loss. But for enlightened risk takers, *risk* also includes opportunities for gain — opportunities that, along with threats of loss, nonprofits should be prepared to manage.

❑ Yes   ❑ No   ❑ Not Sure

Comments: _____

_____

3. There are at least three specific events that, if they happened tomorrow, would be really bad surprises, causing your nonprofit serious loss. Very briefly, and without trying to estimate dollars, these events and the resulting types of loss, would be:

Bad Surprise   Resulting Loss

1. _____   _____

    _____   _____

2. _____   _____

    _____   _____

3. _____   _____

    _____   _____

4.　There are at least three specific events that, if they happened tomorrow, would be really wonderful surprises, offering your nonprofit tremendous opportunities for gain. Very briefly, and without trying to estimate dollars, these events and the resulting opportunities for gain, would be:

<u>Good Surprise</u>　　　　　　　　　　　<u>Resulting Opportunities</u>

1. _____　　_____

2. _____　　_____

3. _____　　_____

5.　Risk is *a measure of the possibility that the future may be surprisingly different from what we expect.* This means you can manage risk by increasing your knowledge so that you can make better predictions and fewer future events will surprise you.

❑ Yes　　　　　❑ No　　　　　❑ Not Sure

Comments: _____

_____

6.　Another way you can manage risk is to broaden your expectations and prepare for a wider range of future events, which reduces the probability that the future will be surprisingly different from what you expect.

❑ Yes　　　　　❑ No　　　　　❑ Not Sure

Comments: _____

_____

7.　By increasing your knowledge and broadening your expectations, you can reduce your uncertainty, becoming more confident in pursuing your nonprofit's goals.

❑ Yes　　　　　❑ No　　　　　❑ Not Sure

Comments: _____

_____

WORKSHEET 1.1   What Risk Means to You (continued)

To Check Your Thinking....

Here is a short case about a particular nonprofit organization. If you were the leader of this nonprofit, how would you answer the questions below?

Mini-Case: Firefighters' Fund Drive

A nonprofit volunteer fire department, whose annual one-month fund drive is scheduled for next October, faces significant downside and upside risks related to the fundraiser. The weather, the state of the economy, the community's fire experience in the three or four months before, and any major news developments (such as a natural disaster, violent crime wave, an epidemic, or a surprise visit to the event by the President of the United States) all may cause the donations the department collects to be much less or much more than last year's donations.

1. What additional knowledge is required to avoid surprises with regard to the fund drive?

Comments: _____

_____

_____

2. How might the fund drive organizers broaden their expectations and prepare for a wider range of future events?

Comments: _____

_____

_____

3. What additional steps can organizers take to gain confidence about undertaking this important fund-raising activity?

Comments: _____

_____

_____

WORKSHEET 1.2 — Why You Manage Risk Here

Enlightened Risk Taking states that a nonprofit organization should manage risk to reduce potential loss and increase potential gains. It also describes five, more specific, reasons for managing risk — to:

1. counter accidental losses by preventing or paying for them;
2. seize opportunities for gain or growth;
3. reduce uncertainty and build confidence within your nonprofit;
4. make your nonprofit a good citizen within your community; and
5. fulfill your nonprofit's community-serving mission.

This is a very general list of strategic risk management objectives. The Center is not saying that all these objectives are valid goals for all nonprofits or that some nonprofits may not have other valid strategic risk management objectives. Nor does the Center suggest a ranking of these objectives in order of importance for any given nonprofit. Only you and your colleagues can do these things for your nonprofit. For this purpose, please consider the following.

1. Does your nonprofit now manage risk for all five of these reasons?

   To counter accidental losses by preventing or paying for them   ❏ Yes   ❏ No
   To seize opportunities for gain or growth   ❏ Yes   ❏ No
   To reduce uncertainty and build confidence within your nonprofit   ❏ Yes   ❏ No
   To make your nonprofit a good citizen within your community   ❏ Yes   ❏ No
   To fulfill your nonprofit's community-serving mission   ❏ Yes   ❏ No

Why or Why Not? Comments: _____

_____

2. Should you add any additional strategic risk management objectives?   ❏ Yes   ❏ No

If yes, indicate additional objectives here: _____

_____

3. Of the strategic risk management objectives that are valid for your nonprofit,
   which one objective is:
   (a) most important? _____
   (b) least important? _____

4. Rank your strategic risk management objectives in the space below.

   1) _____
   2) _____
   3) _____
   4) _____
   5) _____
   6) _____
   7) _____

WORKSHEET 1.3   Dreaming — A Nightmare!

Worksheets 1.3 and 1.4, both about dreaming — actually thoughtful imagining — strive to explore the possibilities of downside and upside risks in your particular nonprofit. Worksheet 1.3 dreams of downside risks, nightmares, by surveying the ways accidental losses and other adverse events can threaten the key assets that empower your nonprofit in working to accomplish its mission. Then Worksheet 1.4 will dream of upside risks where managerial insights lead to innovations and adaptations that increase key assets and help fulfill a nonprofit's mission in unexpectedly wondrous ways.

Worksheet 1.3 aims to display all your nonprofit's downside risks in one chart. Arrayed across the top of this worksheet are the four fundamental types of energizing assets in any nonprofit — its people, property, income and reputation. Listed down the left side of Worksheet 1.3 are two groups of possible causes of loss: 1) accidental losses that have natural, human or economic causes; and 2) adverse changes in a nonprofit's regulatory, market, political, or technological environment that may have surprisingly adverse effects on its ability to carry out its community-serving mission. (You will see in Worksheet 1.4 that these same types of environmental changes also can, in other circumstances, have surprisingly favorable effects on a nonprofit's mission fulfillment.)

Assets / Causes of Loss	(A) People	(B) Property	(C) Income	(D) Reputation
Accidental				
(1) Natural				
(2) Human				
(3) Economic				
Environmental				
(4) Regulatory				
(5) Market				
(6) Political				
(7) Technological				

The lettering of four columns and the numbering of seven rows in the chart help label the individual cells in the chart. To illustrate, cell C3 would include losses of a nonprofit's income due to economic causes of accidental losses.

WORKSHEET 1.3   Dreaming — A Nightmare! (continued)

In principle, every loss that any nonprofit could suffer could be written in a cell in this chart. Damage to an automobile your nonprofit owns could go in several different cells depending on the circumstances. It would go in the Property/Human cell (B2) of this chart if the vehicle were damaged in a roadway accident that was some person's fault. This damage would go in the Property/Natural cell (B1) if the vehicle were swept away in a flood. If damage to this vehicle forced your nonprofit to rent another vehicle until the damaged one could be repaired or replaced, the rental expense would be a loss of net income to your nonprofit. The loss would be charted in the Income/Human cell (C2) if a person caused the original damage, or the Income/Natural cell (C1) if a flood or other natural event had caused the original damage.

Beyond these property and income losses from damage to one of its vehicles, this damage conceivably could occur under circumstances that could bring people and reputation losses upon your nonprofit. For example, one of your board members or your executive director, as an occupant of the vehicle, could have been severely injured when the vehicle was in the roadway accident or damaged by the flood. Or your nonprofit's good reputation also could be tarnished if the vehicle was damaged in a roadway accident that was widely reported as having been the fault of one of your nonprofit's employees who, while driving the vehicle on official business, was privately delivering heroin to several friends. As you can see, a single accident often threatens all four categories of a nonprofit's key assets.

Similarly, adverse changes in regulatory, political, market or technological environments may substantially reduce the effectiveness of your people, property, income and reputation in pursuing your nonprofit's mission. For example, the laws in a growing number of states allow individuals to register their home telephones on do-not-call lists to block unsolicited telemarketing. Thus, the productivity of volunteers assigned to make cold-canvas fund-raising calls for the nonprofit is lessened because the law reduces the size of the market. A technological change that dramatically cuts a nonprofit's property assets might be the development of a medicine that effectively makes obsolete a previous radiological treatment to fight a particular bone disease, thereby making worthless the equipment recently purchased by a single-state nonprofit devoted to eradicating this disease. A change in the nonprofit's marketing environment that might greatly reduce its income would be the creation of a national nonprofit whose mission is to combat all skeletal diseases. The wider geographical reach, broader mission publicity and, perhaps, greater initial funding of this new national organization might seriously jeopardize the income that the older nonprofit was able to generate.

An effective way to identify the specific threats facing your nonprofit is to focus on only one column, one row or one cell of the chart at a time. Each column deals with a category of your nonprofit's key assets; each row deals with one type of accidental or environmental cause of loss; and each cell deals with how one cause-of-loss type could strike one category of your nonprofit's key assets. For example, column A covers all the losses that might strike your nonprofit's people, and row 4 covers all the losses that might arise from adverse regulatory changes. Hence, the earlier example of do-not-call list cutting the effectiveness of a nonprofit's cold canvassing telephone volunteers belongs in cell A4.

You can use this chart of key assets and causes of loss to picture losses that your nonprofit may suffer. You may wish to begin with just one cell in the chart — say, cell B1 — and start by thinking of possible losses to items of your nonprofit's property from natural causes of loss. Here are some suggested steps:

WORKSHEET 1.3   Dreaming — A Nightmare! (continued)

1. Choose one, three or perhaps five specific items of property that your nonprofit owns or uses and consider which of these causes of loss could damage or destroy each of these items of property. The historical loss experiences of your organization or other nonprofits may stir your imagination to predict what nightmarish things could happen.

   _____

   _____

   _____

2. Next, thinking further about these same items of property, give some thought to how the causes of loss you have identified in the chart could injure or damage your nonprofit's people (cell A1), income (cell C1), and reputation (cell D1). More often than not, the same loss-causing event impairs assets in more than one, if not all, of the categories of assets that a nonprofit holds.

   _____

   _____

   _____

3. Continue this thought process with your colleagues using the other cells and rows of the chart, such as human causes of loss in row 2, where theft (including fraud and embezzlement), negligence, and the other human causes of loss may possibly endanger the key people, property, income, and reputation assets of your nonprofit. Drawing on the experiences of other nonprofits that are similar to or geographically near yours may lead you to previously unconsidered loss possibilities.

   _____

   _____

   _____

WORKSHEET 1.3　　　Dreaming — A Nightmare! (continued)

4. As you proceed to the environmental causes of loss, the regulatory, market, political and technological changes again are likely to threaten all of a nonprofit's key assets. For example, if a Congressional (political) or Federal Trade Commission (regulatory) investigation of a nonprofit well known for research to combat a particular disease were to reveal personal misuse of funds by that nonprofit's leaders, all disease-fighting nonprofits would likely suffer losses. Their first losses might well be to their incomes from individual and corporate donations; next might come people losses, as volunteers and high-profile board members, whose pride and recognition from affiliation with disease-focused nonprofits changed to embarrassment and stigma.

_____

_____

_____

_____

_____

_____

_____

_____

_____

WORKSHEET 1.3   Dreaming — A Nightmare! (continued)

5. To complete these nightmare scenarios you have developed in the separate cells, rows and columns of the chart, imagine what could happen if the events in several different parts of the chart were to begin happening at the same time. What if … Your headquarters is hit by a 100-year flood the same week that a court awards a $3 million verdict against your nonprofit because one of your van drivers was negligent two years ago. What if … Earlier the same month, the corporation whose unrestricted grants accounted for 20 percent of your operating budget went bankrupt and the state's attorney general announced an investigation into whether your nonprofit's sale of a large block of this donor company's stock two days before its bankruptcy was announced constitutes illegal insider trading. In response to this avalanche of bad news, your board chairman resigns.

Is all this impossible? No. Very unlikely? Of course. Surprising? Probably. But not as surprising as it might have been before you started *The Workbook*. Is this the devastating demise of your nonprofit — the end of its mission? Not if you begin to practice *Enlightened Risk Taking*.

WORKSHEET 1.4   If You Could Dream of Paradise...

Just as you can suffer terrible dreams, you can cherish wondrous ones. Indeed, strategic risk management requires you to have both bad and good dreams, to remember both types and, as far as you can, to prepare for all possibilities.

So Worksheet 1.4 turns the tables on Worksheet 1.3, focusing on wonderfully surprising events that — if you are alert enough to see them and adequately prepared to seize the opportunity — can really advance your nonprofit toward achieving its mission.

As shown in the columns of the following chart, you will still dream of your key assets: people, property, income and reputation. The rows of this new chart deal with causes for surprising gains rather than losses. Recall from *Enlightened Risk Taking* that managerial insight is the fundamental wellspring of opportunities for surprising, *breakthrough* gains that can materialize within your nonprofit as either innovations, or creative adaptations of ideas originated by others. Therefore, this new surprising opportunities for gain chart for Worksheet 1.4 has two rows, one for each fundamental cause of gain.

Assets / Causes of Gain	(A) People	(B) Property	(C) Income	(D) Reputation
(1) Innovations				
(2) Adaptations				

True innovations that originate within your nonprofit can greatly enhance any or all of your key assets; thus these innovations may fit into any or all of the A1 through D1 cells. The adaptations (borrowing and creatively changing others' ideas) can be stimulated by any change in any factor in a nonprofit's environment (regulatory, market, political, or technological), and an adaptation (like an innovation) may greatly increase any or all of a nonprofit's key assets.

As you consider the questions on page 13, do not struggle over which cell in the chart is the best location for any particular idea you generate. The purpose of the chart is to stimulate thought, not to confine it. Furthermore, developing a full list of gain-generating innovations and adaptations is not as easy as making a chart of causes of accidental losses. Your knowledge of causes of losses is largely accumulated history; innovations and adaptations are new, out of the ordinary creations at a particular time and place that cannot be charted in advance.

WORKSHEET 1.4   If You Could Dream of Paradise... (continued)

Still, as an example, consider past innovations and adaptations, or imagine new ones.

Consider:

1. What amazingly wonderful things conceivably could happen to greatly increase the mission-centered effectiveness of:
    (a) any two specific persons or categories of people who devote their energy to your nonprofit?

    _____

    _____

    (b) any three specific items or types of property your nonprofit uses or owns?

    _____

    _____

    _____

    (c) any three significant sources of your nonprofit's income?

    _____

    _____

    _____

    (d) your nonprofit's reputation with two of its major constituencies?

    _____

    _____

[Note: The various parts of this question let you generate up to 10 different wondrously surprising, opportunity-filled, events. If you and your colleagues cannot think of 10 wonderful surprises, work with whatever lesser number of events you do generate and try to trace the potential positive effects of each event on all four categories of your nonprofit's key assets.]

2. The surprising events you described in answer to the previous question generated opportunities for your nonprofit to move forward remarkably toward fulfilling its mission. For one of the five surprising events, ask:
    (a) What specific opportunities would that event, if it happened tomorrow, present to your nonprofit?

    _____

    (b) What specific key assets — people, property, income and reputation — would your nonprofit need to have tomorrow to fully seize that opportunity?

    _____

    (c) How is your nonprofit fully prepared for the opportunities tomorrow may bring?

    _____

    _____

Enlightened Risk Taking combines definitions of *risk* and *management* to define *strategic risk management* as *planning, organizing, directing and controlling the resources and activities of an organization in order to enable that organization to strive for its full potential — countering potential losses and seizing potential gains — even though the future may be surprisingly different from what we expect.* Do not be alarmed if this still does not seem familiar.

Strategic risk management is today a leading-edge concept. Sixty years ago, there was virtually nothing called risk management, and certainly nothing called *strategic risk management.* Sixty years ago, students and practitioners of management paid no conscious attention to risk — downside or upside — and, if they privately felt any uncertainty, they bought some insurance, tried to ignore these feelings and just pushed honorably ahead with their plans. If this is what your nonprofit still faithfully does, that is fine. Nonetheless, your reading *The Workbook* indicates that you and your nonprofit want to do more about risk, both downside and upside, to better fulfill your nonprofit's mission.

About 40 years ago, traditional risk management was born. It sprang from managers of profit-seeking firms recognizing that so-called *accidents* such as employee injuries, roadway crashes, slips and falls, and building fires, really were not that accidental. More and more these managers realized that over time, these events impose predictable costs on an organization. These accident costs are manageable; they can be reduced by preventing accidents and by finding more cost-effective ways of financing recovery from mishaps that cannot be prevented. Instead of insuring against everything, a nonprofit that manages risk in a traditional sense takes on (*assumes* or *retains*) some exposures to accidental losses through *deductible* clauses in its insurance policies and even *self-insuring* against some losses by calling upon the nonprofit's reserves or operating funds when needed. Perhaps this *traditional* risk management of downside risk is what your nonprofit now does, maybe independently or jointly with some other nonprofits. If so, congratulations!

The next step is the emerging practice of strategic risk management, which encompasses both downside risks of accidental losses and upside risks of potential gains. Strategic risk management, which originated in the investment and banking communities perhaps five or 10 years ago, focuses on upside opportunities for gain, treating the expenses associated with downside risks of accidental loss as necessary costs that must be borne in order to benefit from taking promising upside risks.

Where your nonprofit rests along this risk management spectrum is part of the context of your organization that you will examine in the next section of *The Workbook.* For now, however, to better understand what strategic risk management can do for your nonprofit, consider, or better discuss with your colleagues, whether you agree with the following statements:

Do You Agree That...?

1. Within your nonprofit's management and leadership team, you should think and talk about risk and uncertainty more than you do now.   ❑ Yes   ❑ No   ❑ Not Sure

Comments: _____

_____

WORKSHEET 1.5   **From None, to Traditional, to Strategic (continued)**

2. When you do think or talk about risk or uncertainty, it is usually about downside threats of loss, not upside opportunities for gain.

☐ Yes   ☐ No   ☐ Not Sure

Comments: _____

_____

_____

3. You currently practice:
    (a) essentially no risk management, or
    (b) some traditional risk management, or
    (c) strategic risk management.

Circle your choice and explain it in the space below.

_____

_____

_____

4. You need to raise your nonprofit's level of risk management practice. Why?

☐ Yes   ☐ No   ☐ Not Sure

Comments: _____

_____

_____

CHAPTER 1

Establish the Context

Our work to this point — defining strategic risk management and looking briefly at what it now means in your organization — has set the stage for what may well be applying the strategic risk management process to your nonprofit. The first of the five steps in that process is establishing a specific organizational context for applying this process. You have already seen part of that context through Worksheet 1.5, simply by considering how often risk is discussed within your nonprofit's leadership and what it means when it is discussed. Whatever those discussions have been (even if there have never been any), they are the baseline from which progress toward strategic risk management must begin.

This chapter contains four worksheets that focus on establishing the context for strategic risk management for your nonprofit. To establish the context of your nonprofit's future strategic risk management efforts, your past experiences with accidents are important primarily because they set the tone for how you are likely to do and to feel when future accidents occur. (What you did well in the past, you can do well again. The things that really scared you in the past would still be scary if they happened again.) You want to be sure not to repeat any mistakes you made last time there was an accident. While it is true that any nonprofit's accident experience gives some clues about the accidental losses it may suffer in the future, there are much better, more statistically reliable, sources of information for appraising a nonprofit's accidental loss exposures. Your organization's collective psychological and managerial responses to its past accidents are especially important in shaping its readiness for any similar future accidents.

WORKSHEET 1.6 Your Experience With Accidents

1. The following chart gives a framework for gathering some historical loss information and sorting the organizational responses. This chart is best used to structure a group discussion of your nonprofit's accidental losses over perhaps the last five years, bringing together a few basic facts about each accident, how it could have been prevented, and how (if at all) that accident changed or still affects your nonprofit's activities. For now, your concern should not be with how much the accident cost, or who may have been at fault. Rather, think about how that accident has influenced the way your nonprofit functions today, how that accident helped establish — for better or worse — the context for your nonprofit's readiness for a similar accident tomorrow.

Event	What Happened?	The Cause(s)?	How Has This Event Changed Your Nonprofit?

This chart may have more or fewer rows than you need for the number of significant accidental losses your nonprofit has experienced in the last five years. In working with it, remember that — to establish the strategic risk management context for your nonprofit — a seemingly small accident that changes attitudes or behaviors may be much more significant than another accident that cost a lot of money but had no lasting influence on your operations or attitudes toward risk.

2.   Are you or your colleagues aware of any instances within your nonprofit in which a very severe and costly accidental loss has had little, if any, effect on your nonprofit's normal ways of operating or management's attitude toward risk?

❑ Yes   ❑ No

Comments: _____

_____

3.   Are you or your colleagues aware of any instances within your nonprofit in which a relatively minor and not especially costly accidental loss has greatly changed your nonprofit's normal ways of operating or management's attitude toward risk?

❑ Yes   ❑ No

Comments: _____

_____

4.   Within your nonprofit, what factors — other than the dollar cost of an accidental loss — appear to determine the effects that an accidental loss is likely to have on your nonprofit's normal ways of operating or management's attitude toward risk?

Comments: _____

_____

5.   In retrospect, have your nonprofit's past responses to accidental losses generally been (a) appropriate, or (b) inappropriate for dealing with threats of comparable future accidental losses?

❑ Appropriate ❑ Inappropriate

Comments: _____

_____

Your nonprofit's experience with upside risks, capitalizing on opportunities for gain, is as important to the strategic risk management context within your organization as its experience with unexpected accidental losses. Therefore, Worksheet 1.7 develops a perspective opposite to that of Worksheet 1.6, looking at your nonprofit's history of dealing with opportunities for gain — originating new innovations or adapting others' new ideas to your nonprofit's particular situation. As with downside threats of accidental losses, your objective in reviewing your nonprofit's experience with opportunities for gain will be to look for patterns in the opportunities your nonprofit has recognized, your responses to those opportunities and how your responses have affected your likely responses to similar future opportunities.

In your thinking and in discussions with your colleagues, please note one very crucial difference between upside opportunities and downside accidents: accidents usually are fairly easy to recognize, opportunities are often fairly difficult to spot. (Remember in strategic risk management, managerial insight is the fundamental source of opportunities. People lacking this insight may well not see actual opportunities for innovation or adaptation that other, more perceptive people may recognize.) Some of your colleagues will see opportunities where others, perhaps you, see none. Seeing what others do not is one of the essential features of upside risk, as Columbus could have told you when he was canvassing Europe for a monarch to finance his first voyage to discover the New World.

Some of your colleagues — perhaps even you — may be reluctant to actively consider looking for upside risks of opportunities for growth. They, or you, may truly feel that the fiduciary obligations that the law imposes on officers and employees of a nonprofit organization require that, above all, they must preserve and protect the assets and income of your nonprofit, not take any chances whatever to grow these assets and income. In this view, preservation, not growth, may be not *just* the most important — but instead the *only* — proper goal of those entrusted with managing a nonprofit's resources. For them, knowingly taking risks in hopes of gain is appropriate for profit-seeking executives — but not for the leaders of nonprofits who are charged with a public trust to carry out a nonprofit mission. Choosing to take risks, even to just increase the productivity of a nonprofit's resources seemingly without exposing these resources to the threat of loss, may be contrary to some of your leaders' understanding of their duties to your nonprofit and to its mission. Others, perhaps you, may believe that the overriding obligation of a nonprofit's leaders is to the future of its mission, not to its present resources. For them, taking reasonable risks to enhance their nonprofit's resources to fulfill that mission in an uncertain world is the foremost fiduciary duty of a nonprofit's leaders.

There may be no clear resolution of these contending views as you discuss with your colleagues how your nonprofit has dealt with upside risks in the recent past and how you may handle them in the future. Resolving any differing attitudes toward upside (or downside) risks within yourself or among your colleagues is not essential just now. However, *recognizing* any such differences now is crucial, because these differences, or any contrasts in your perhaps differing approaches to upside versus downside risks, is important to establishing the context within which your nonprofit undertakes strategic risk management.

WORKSHEET 1.7   Your Experiences Innovating and Adapting

The Opportunity	Your Response (if any)	How Has Your Response Changed Your Nonprofit?

1. In general, does it appear that your nonprofit has done well in recognizing opportunities for gain when they arose, as opposed to (a) failing to see opportunities that really were there, and (b) imagining opportunities that, in retrospect, really did not exist at the time?

Comments: _____

_____

2. In the situations where your nonprofit's leaders have been correct in recognizing opportunities and moving to capitalize on them, (a) what have you done very well? and (b) what could you have done better?

Comments: _____

_____

3. Has the past five (or 10) years' experience with upside risks made your nonprofit (a) more willing and better prepared or (b) less willing and less prepared to seize opportunities for gain?

Comments: _____

_____

4. If Columbus walked into your headquarters tomorrow with a proposal for reaching a *New World* where your nonprofit's mission could readily be accomplished, would you *seriously consider* financing the voyage?

Comments: _____

On either the downside or the upside, dealing with risk can be a tricky, often scary thing. Whether buying insurance or a new building, negotiating the settlement of a legal claim or the rental of a theater for a special event, or searching for an appropriate mutual fund investment or an adequate fire-suppression system, the leaders of many for-profits recognize that these important decisions involve knowledge and skills that often are beyond their own. Faced with the risks and uncertainties inherent in these situations, many nonprofit executives quite sensibly seek out and rely on outside experts. How well such experts have served them in the past greatly influences how willingly and confidently these leaders will turn to other outside experts when dealing with threats of accidental loss or opportunities for unexpected gains. Their past experiences with outside experts when confronting risky situations is an important element of the context within which they will strategically manage risk in the future.

If experts outside your immediate organizational family — the lawyers, accountants, insurance professionals, safety specialists, and other consultants — whom your nonprofit has hired in the past to guide you in making major risk-laden decisions typically have given you good results, your level of comfort with the strategic risk management process will be much greater than if these outsiders have typically let you down. Or perhaps your nonprofit usually has had good luck with some types of experts — such as accountants and organizational development consultants — but bad luck with others.

To understand how these experiences may affect your future working relationships with the outside experts you may need to implement strategic risk management within your nonprofit, consider the chart on the next page. The first column lists several types of outside experts with special knowledge or skills upon which your nonprofit may want to call in coping with upside or downside risks. In the second column, you should note the experts you have worked with and describe very briefly the types of work they have done for your nonprofit. The next column gives you space to indicate whether your experience with each expert was generally good, poor or indifferent (G, P, or I). The last column gives you space to sketch some thoughts about reasons why your experience with each expert went particularly well or poorly.

WORKSHEET 1.8 — Your Experiences Working With Outside Experts

TYPE OF EXPERT	Work Done	Rating (G/P/I)	Reasons for Rating
Safety Consultant			
Insurance Sales			
Insurance Claims			
Insurance Consultant			
Employee Benefits			
Attorney			
Financial Consultant			
Accountant/CPA			
Strategic Planning			
Other			

The most important column in this chart is the last, the one dealing with the reasons your work with outside experts went well or poorly. Where you worked well together, identify how or why; you will want to repeat or maintain these favorable factors in your future dealings with outside experts. Where your working relationship was poor, search diligently for the real reasons for the failures. Ask yourself and your colleagues whether there is anything you could have done to have converted failures into successes. The faults you can find, particularly any faults within your own nonprofit, may be your keys to success in the future.

Those who wish to accomplish much must first expect much of themselves. If you expect much, you can possibly accomplish even more; if you expect little, you will surely accomplish even less. Thus, a most crucial element of the context in which your nonprofit manages risk is the expectations your nonprofit — everyone who labors to achieve its mission — expects to accomplish through wisely managing both downside and upside risks.

Enlightened Risk Taking sets forth a lofty overall goal for strategic risk management in any nonprofit: to enable the organization to strive for its full potential by countering risks of accidental loss and seizing opportunities for gain. Within this overall goal, strategic risk management seeks:

❑ to prevent or finance recovery from threats of loss; and
❑ to identify and pursue promising opportunities for gain.

To help you and your colleagues recognize, express and share your basic views on how important strategic risk management is to your nonprofit's success, please consider the following questions:

1. Within the last three to five years, has your nonprofit faced major difficulties because it has not been able to cost-effectively:

a. prevent accidental losses from impairing its key people, property, income and reputation assets?
❑ Yes ❑ No

Comments _____

_____

b. finance recovery from significant accidental losses to these key assets? ❑ Yes ❑ No

Comments _____

_____

c. identify opportunities to make innovations or adaptations that would greatly enhance your nonprofit's key assets? ❑ Yes ❑ No

Comments _____

_____

d. pursue these opportunities, once they have been identified, with appropriate people, property, income or reputation resources?   ❑ Yes ❑ No

Comments _____

_____

2. To what extent, if at all, have any of the difficulties you mentioned in answering the previous questions hampered your nonprofit's efforts within the last three to five years to fulfill its community-serving mission? Answer with as many specific examples as you can.

Comments: _____

_____

_____

_____

3. Listed below are several pairs of general strategic risk management goals. Within each pair, which of the two goals is likely to be more important to your nonprofit's successful pursuit of its mission during the next three to five years (circle your answer)? Try to give reasons for your answers in the space provided.

❏ Countering threats of accidental loss or seizing opportunities for gain?

Reasons: _____

_____

❏ Preventing accidental losses or financing recovery from such losses?

Reasons: _____

_____

❏ Identifying opportunities to grow your nonprofit's resources in insightful ways or finding the resources with which to pursue these opportunities?

Reasons: _____

_____

4. Reconsidering each of the choices you made between pairs of goals in question 3, can you imagine any surprising circumstances in which the goal you did *not* choose might turn out to be the more important one of the pair? Explain.

Comments: _____

_____

_____

Who Will Champion Risk Management?

Who is in the best position to champion strategic risk management in a nonprofit? Many organizations have taken the position that "our insurance professional handles risk management." If you think of risk management as a discipline that integrates mathematical analysis with legal issues and contracting, it is not surprising to want someone else to *handle it*. But if you think of risk management as necessary to protecting your nonprofit's critical assets (people, property, income and reputation) and empowering an organization to achieve its mission, then the idea of relying on outsiders to manage risk may be unthinkable.

Deciding how to structure the risk management function in your nonprofit is no easy task. Some of the alternatives and the things you may want to take into consideration follow.

Fully Staffed Function

Several hundred nonprofits across the country have chosen to hire a full-time risk manager to coordinate risk management activities for the organization. This approach seems to be most popular in organizations that:

❑ manage long-standing, complex insurance programs for their affiliates or chapters that include assuming some risk (through a captive insurer or large retentions);
❑ coordinate loss control and claims handling for a network of affiliates;
❑ operate intensive on-site recreational programs, such as a swimming program;
❑ deliver health-care services in a clinic or hospital setting;
❑ provide residential care for youth, the elderly or persons with developmental disabilities; or
❑ operate as umbrella entities for large religious denominations.

Some of the advantages of this approach include:

❏ the symbolic effect of making risk management a staff position at the organization;

❏ ensuring that someone is available on a full-time basis to respond to risk management questions and issues as they arise;

❏ providing a point person or department for risk management vendors, such as insurance consultants and brokers;

❏ ensuring greater consistency with respect to post-incident or post-accident reporting and record keeping;

❏ sending a signal to individuals throughout the organization that indicates the importance of risk management to the organization; and

❏ ensuring staff leadership and coordination for a function that will undoubtedly involve some volunteers.

Some of the downsides of this approach include the risk that:

❏ individuals throughout the organization will view risk management as *someone else's* responsibility;

❏ risk management will be viewed as a subset of finance rather than as an over-arching discipline; and

❏ the risk management unit will be undervalued in the organization due to the difficulty of demonstrating and appraising losses that were prevented or avoided as a result of this unit's activities.

The potential downsides can all be addressed if an organization recognizes them and takes appropriate action.

All Volunteer Risk Management Committee

At the other end of the spectrum from hiring a full-time risk management professional is an organization that has chosen to vest responsibility for risk management in a volunteer risk management committee. This approach is most popular in all-volunteer nonprofits, or those with very small paid staffs. Some of the advantages of this approach include:

❏ engaging individuals with a diverse skills set in the process of identifying a nonprofit's risks and strategic responses;

❏ sharing responsibility for risk management among members of a team; and

❏ reducing the possibility that the departure or absence of one individual would derail an organization's risk management program.

Some of the disadvantages of this approach include:

❏ the lack of paid staff available to support volunteer efforts on behalf of the nonprofit;

❏ the inability of expertise to accumulate as membership on the committee rotates;

❏ putting too heavy a burden on a group of volunteers;

❑ the difficulty of ensuring a consistent approach to record keeping or policy development without professional coordination; and

❑ the possibility that the committee will be dominated by insurance professionals whose interests may at some point conflict with the nonprofit's interests.

Once again, with time spent reflecting on these concerns, the disadvantages of this approach can be managed.

Something in Between

Many nonprofits will organize the function somewhere in between the two approaches described. They might use both a full-time or part-time risk manager plus a risk management committee to obtain the benefits of both approaches. Or they might use a risk management committee, but include one or more paid staff as committee members. It is important to:

❑ design an approach that recognizes the strengths, weaknesses, culture, circumstances and needs of your organization;

❑ formulate a strategy that is sustainable in your organization — do not establish a framework that will not work due to asset (human, financial and other) constraints; and

❑ strive always to involve people throughout the organization in the process of identifying and addressing risks.

More About Risk Management Committees

A risk management committee is a group of people charged with developing and overseeing an organization's risk management program. The committee has three primary responsibilities:

1. identify the organization's exposures;
2. develop a risk control program; and
3. establish a risk financing strategy.

Who staffs your risk management committee will depend on your organization's operations and unique risks. For example, a nonprofit health clinic's risk management committee may include medical personnel, an attorney, an insurance professional, and a member of the administrative staff. In contrast, a nonprofit mentoring program serving at-risk youth may include the volunteer coordinator, a volunteer mentor, an attorney, and an insurance professional on its committee.

A nonprofit should try to tap people with a range of expertise and first-hand knowledge of the organization's operations. Forming a risk management committee that includes both employees and volunteers will ensure that both broad and unique perspectives are applied to risk-identification, while encouraging creative problem solving.

The most effective committee will include people with knowledge of and experience with the nonprofit's operations, future programming plans, legal structure and operating procedures.

What are the Committee's Core Responsibilities?

The risk management committee is responsible for all phases of an organization's risk management program — from development through implementation and monitoring. If your nonprofit employs a full-time risk manager or has designated a staff liaison for risk management, that individual generally coordinates the activities of the risk management committee.

Once the organization decides to establish a risk management committee, the first step is to select the members of the committee. The members then create a work plan for developing and implementing the organization's risk management program. The work plan will spell out the committee's ongoing responsibilities, which may include any or all of the following:

- ❑ developing, for board approval, an organizational risk management policy that affirms the organization's commitment to safeguarding its assets.
- ❑ establishing the nonprofit's risk management goals (for example, ensuring its survival, maintaining essential operations or providing humanitarian services).
- ❑ identifying the organization's risks and establishing the risk management priorities.
- ❑ selecting the best risk management techniques (avoidance, modification, retention or sharing) for the priority risks.
- ❑ recommending appropriate risk financing alternatives.
- ❑ communicating the agency's risk management plan and loss control procedures to the board of directors, employees, volunteers, clients and the other stakeholders.
- ❑ selecting an insurance advisor (a broker, agent or consultant) and negotiating insurance arrangements.
- ❑ overseeing loss prevention and control activities.
- ❑ providing an annual risk management report to the board of directors.

Making the Case for Risk Management in Your Nonprofit

Support for risk management activities should begin with the board of directors. If your board does not believe risk management is critical to the success of the organization, then the first order of business is to demonstrate to the board how risk management can protect the vital assets of the nonprofit and enable it to achieve its ambitious mission. A nonprofit board not only establishes policies that govern operations, it models behavior for the organization's paid and volunteer staff, clients, and other constituencies. When the board attaches significance to a particular issue, it is likely that the staff and other people will follow suit.

Without sacrificing program goals or a nonprofit's enthusiasm for new activities, the board can and should demonstrate to others that risk management frees up — rather than consumes — resources for the agency's community-serving mission. The board can dispel some of the misconceptions about risk management through its actions and policies.

The board has a number of ways to start modeling a commitment to risk management. First, the board should encourage key operational units to factor risk management into their activities. For example, the department responsible for special events should consider and address the risks associated with hosting the annual 10K fund-raiser. The human resources manager should consider the risks of a wrongful termination action when proposing a progressive discipline policy to the personnel committee. The development director should consider the possible backlash that might result from accepting sponsorship funds from the liquor industry. The board should direct its attention to the precautions and steps to be taken to ensure that its own affairs are conducted in a legal and appropriate manner, as well as ask questions to fulfill its fiduciary responsibility to protect the organization and its assets.

Some of the questions the board might ask include:

❑ How does the board model its commitment to safety and risk management? What actions convey its importance to the nonprofit's constituencies?
❑ What are the risks associated with this activity or program?
❑ Can we conduct this activity or program safely?
❑ If no, what alternative activity would have similar results without the unacceptable risks?
❑ What resources or actions do we need to take to ensure the safety of participants, staff and the general public?

WORSHEET 2.1   Risk Management Committee Selection Worksheet

Organization: _____

Categories of Expertise

Committee Member	Insurance/ Finance	Legal	Operations	Volunteer Programs	Other (describe)

WORKSHEET 2.2   Risk Management Projects/Tasks

Organization: _____

Date: _____

Task	Leader	Start/Finish Dates
Risk Identification		
Review Subcommittee Findings		
Establish Priorities		
Evaluate and Select Techniques		
Document the Program		

CHAPTER 3

Appraise Your Risks

Having established the context for strategic risk management in your nonprofit, you now proceed to the second step in the strategic risk management process: appraising your nonprofit's risks — both the downside risks from threats of accidental losses and the upside risks of opportunities for gains. As explained in Chapter 3 of *Enlightened Risk Taking*, appraising risks involves (1) identifying both threats of loss and opportunities for gain and (2) prioritizing these threats and opportunities to see which of them deserve special attention because of their relatively high probability, high potential magnitude, and great variability. You may want to refer to *Enlightened Risk Taking* as you and your colleagues work with the upcoming worksheets because they relate directly to some of the diagrams and charts in that book. These worksheets treat downside and upside risks equally even though your nonprofit may from time to time shift greater emphasis to either downside threats or upside opportunities, depending on your leaders' changing attitudes toward risk, your nonprofit's recent experiences, or general economic conditions.

WORSHEET 3.1   Where Your Key Assets Lie

The key assets of all community-serving nonprofits lie in their people, property, income and reputation. Because nonprofits are so diverse, each nonprofit has a virtually unique set of individuals, properties, sources of income, and elements of its reputation that are the sources of its key assets. Therefore, you cannot begin with a set list of people, items of real or personal (tangible or intangible) property, types or specific sources of income, or qualities that build reputations that would be meaningful for each nonprofit.

Instead, the people who know your nonprofit best need to make their own list of key assets for the organization. The following chart aims to help you start building your list. The chart is only the start of your list because it has spaces for only five specific assets in each of the four asset categories, a total of 20 assets.

In the categories where your nonprofit has many assets, select the top five — perhaps based not so much on their dollar value as the criticality to your nonprofit's mission. In categories where you have few mission-critical assets, try to find at least three. In selecting the assets for your specific nonprofit, be aware that this chart is the start of an extensive exercise through which you can begin practicing strategic risk management within your nonprofit. For each of the assets in your nonprofit that you identify here, the worksheets that follow will track for (1) threats of accidental loss and opportunities for amazing growth, (2) strategic risk management alternatives for countering these losses and seizing these opportunities; (3) making choices among these alternatives, (4) taking action on these choices, and (5) following up on and adjusting these actions. Here you begin applying what you have studied.

Key Asset Categories	People	Property	Income	Reputation
Specific Examples				
First Key Asset				
Second Key Asset				
Third Key Asset				
Fourth Key Asset				
Fifth Key Asset				

WORKSHEET 3.2   Prioritizing Threats of Loss

With many threats of loss and opportunities for gain to manage, and perhaps limited resources — especially limited managerial time — to devote to managing them, you should direct these scarce resources first to the most extreme risks: the worst of the threats and the best of the opportunities. Chapter 3 of *Enlightened Risk Taking* offers two scales for finding the most extreme threats or opportunities for ranking these downside and upside risks so that that the most threatening potential losses and the most promising potential gains get priority treatment. One scale is quantitative, the other qualitative.

Both scales rank threats or opportunities by the probability (or likelihood) and magnitude (dollars of loss or gain) of the uncertain events that these risks may generate. The higher the probability and the greater the magnitude, the higher the priority. For the quantitative scale, assign a value from 1 to 10 to the probability of each threat or opportunity and another value from 1 to 10 for the magnitude of each threat or opportunity and add the two numbers together, getting an overall score for each threat or opportunity. Thus, a threat or opportunity with very high probability and very high magnitude might score 20, while another risk might score 2 (1 for probability plus 1 for magnitude). All threats and opportunities are ranked, prioritized by their total scores. The ones with the higher scores get the greater, more prompt risk management attention.

Under the qualitative scale, the rankings are simpler but arguably more subjective. Both probability and magnitude are rated High, Medium or Low. (This three-value scoring has the advantage of reducing possible differences of opinion among your colleagues as to whether, under the quantitative scale, a given threat or opportunity rates a 6 or a 7 for probability or magnitude.) By this qualitative scale, a threat or opportunity that is given a High/Medium rating has priority over a threat or opportunity that receives a Medium/Medium rating.

By either the quantitative or the qualitative ranking system, two threats or two opportunities may receive equal ratings. In these *tie* situations, at least for threats of accidental loss, the threat with the higher magnitude normally should be given priority because large accidental losses, even if few in number, typically are more devastating than a larger number of smaller losses. If two opportunities receive equal ratings, it usually is strictly up to management's intuition as to which of the two opportunities should be undertaken first. If a threat and an opportunity have equal ratings, the conservative, fiduciary climate that quite properly prevails in most nonprofits normally gives priority to the threat — the equally rated opportunity typically would *wait until later* for senior management attention.

For the moment, your strategic risk management focus is on threats of accidental loss to your nonprofit. You will get to opportunities for gain shortly. Working with your colleagues, refer to the set of threats of accidental loss that you developed in Worksheet 3.1. Discuss the probability and magnitude of the losses that these may generate, using only the quantitative rating scales. (If you cannot agree on, for example, whether a given risk should be rated 6 or 7 for, say, probability, take a vote or an average — 6.5 in this case.) Then insert your findings into the following table, filling as many rows as you had specific risks in Table 3.1.

WORSHEET 3.2	Prioritizing Threats of Loss

Rank	Description of Threat	Probability (Frequency) Score	Magnitude Score	Total Score
1				
2				
3				
4				
5				
6				
7				
8				
9				
10				
11				
12				
13				
14				
15				
16				
17				
18				
19				
20				

Completing this chart may be hard work for you alone or for you and your colleagues. The most difficult part probably was the process. But your hard work will pay dividends as you next apply the same process on the other side of strategic risk management, the surprising opportunities for remarkable gains.

WORKSHEET 3.3   **Prioritizing Opporunities to Grow Your Key Assets**

Opportunities for growth need to be prioritized in the same ways and for the same reasons as threats of accidental loss — so that strategic risk management can give the highest priority to the opportunities that have the greatest probability of generating the greatest leaps forward for your nonprofit. Therefore, in the table following, list opportunities for surprising growth. You can use the same quantitative or qualitative ratings you used in Worksheet 3.2 (prioritizing threats of accidental loss), for gauging the probability and magnitude of success for these opportunities. Then rank the opportunities based on their total score. Indicate the rank you assign in the first column.

Rank	Description of Opportunity	Probability Score	Magnitude Score	Total Score

In Worksheets 3.2 and 3.3, you developed prioritized lists of downside and upside risks — of threats of accidental losses and opportunities for insightful gains within your nonprofit. Within the strategic risk management process, you are now ready to make choices and take action.

CHAPTER 4

Decide What to Do

Within the context of *The Workbook*, the options from which you and your colleagues must decide involve as many as 20 downside and up to 15 upside risks. For the downside risks, your options are one or more of the risk management techniques described in Chapters 3 and 4 of *Enlightened Risk Taking*. Chapter 3 presents the full spectrum of risk management techniques, and Chapter 4 delves more deeply into the technical aspects of loss prevention. For the upside risks, your options are (1) to take the risk by seizing the opportunity, perhaps incorporating various risk management techniques to minimize potential negatives or (2) reject the risk by declining the opportunity.

To help you practice — and hopefully gain confidence — about strategic risk management decision-making, *The Workbook* and the following worksheets actually simplify the real world. They simplify it by asking you to deal with no more than 40 risks (reality confronts you with many more), by offering only a limited number of distinct techniques for treating these risks, and by largely ignoring combinations of any number of separate techniques applied simultaneously. Even with these simplifications, strategic risk management decision-making can become exciting, especially when it involves your nonprofit.

WORKSHEET 4.1   Alternatives for Threats of Loss

The first step in deciding what to do is to lay out your options. The next chart enables you to do just that for the five threats of accidental loss to which you and your colleagues gave the highest priority in Worksheet 3.2. The far-left column of the following chart lists the risk management techniques described in *Enlightened Risk Taking,* beginning with the theories of accident causation and prevention presented in Chapter 4. The remaining columns of this chart give you space to describe, briefly, the five threats of accidental loss that deserve the highest priority for your nonprofit.

Threat / Theory/Technique	Threat #1	Threat #2	Threat #3	Threat #4	Threat #5
Domino Theory					
General Methods of Control					
System Safety Approach					
Avoidance					
Loss Prevention					
Loss Reduction					
Segregation of Exposures					
Contractual Sharing					
Training					
Safety Equipment					
Limits, Rules, Requirements					
Screen Staff, Volunteers, Participants					
Supervise					
Program Design Changes					
Equipment Maintenance					
Develop Crisis Management Plan					
Make Expectations Clear					
Obtain Outside Help					
Inventory Assets					
Comply With Applicable Laws					
Implement Workable Internal Controls					
Prepare to Pay for Some Accidental Losses					

WORKSHEET 4.1   **Alternatives for Threats of Loss (continued)**

For each of the five high-priority threats in this chart, consider how appropriate (or inappropriate) each of the risk management techniques listed down the left column would be in managing that threat. Use a ranking of *4* for very appropriate and *0* for not appropriate at all. Enter a *1, 2, or 3* for techniques that would have intermediate degrees of appropriateness. When you and you colleagues have completed this chart, you will have some clear ideas about which risk management techniques are vital in coping with your greatest threat of accidental loss.

One further point is crucial. The risk management technique at the very bottom of the chart — Prepare to Pay for Some Accidental Losses — should be filled in for each of the five threats. Despite all the possible risk management techniques that come before paying for losses, some accidents are bound to occur. If your nonprofit is to survive a loss with financial implications, you need to prepare. Arranging proper risk financing for potentially major accidental losses is often a complex task for which almost every organization's leaders need to call on outside help, even if an organization plans to pay for the losses itself. In any case, some contingency plans to pay some losses are essential.

WORKSHEET 4.2   Alternatives for Opportunities for Gain

The risks associated with innovative and adaptive insightful opportunities for gains may at first appear to be fundamentally different from the risks associated with threats of accidental loss. You may think that you *must* deal with threats of accidental loss, but you can *choose* to ignore opportunities for gain. This conclusion, however, is misleading. Although it is possible to dispell some threats of accidental loss by totally avoiding the assets and activities that give rise to these threats, those might be the very assets and activities that are essential to your nonprofit's mission. For instance, a child day-care center cannot operate without participants. And despite the various precautions taken by the day-care center, from constructing playgrounds that meet or exceed the Consumer Product Safety Commission's standards to thoroughly screening teachers and administrative personnel, a young client may suffer an accidental or intentional injury.

Thus, with respect to downside risks, the board of the day-care center recognizes the importance of taking reasonable steps to protect the nonprofit's young clients, while still providing a nurturing environment that includes outdoor play areas, enthusiastic teachers, and various forms of play equipment. The day-care center also knows that it needs to have resources set aside or insurance policies available that will pay for the harm suffered by a client despite all of the precautions the nonprofit has taken. The board further realizes that the center must be innovative to set itself apart and compete for clients in a rapidly growing community. To do so, the center decides to convert a barn on its 10-acre property as a *petting farm* for the children. The center purchases a range of animals, hires a staff member to care for the animals, and schedules daily visits to the "petting farm" for each class of children at the center.

Worksheet 4.2 helps you look at your strategic risk management choices for the opportunities for gain that you rated earlier in Worksheet 3.3. In the second column of the following chart, identify the five opportunities to which you gave the highest priorities in Worksheet 3.3. Also, in the second column, describe some of the downside risks of pursuing the opportunity and steps the nonprofit can take to counter these. In the third column, describe what effect you and your colleagues believe your not seizing this opportunity sometime within the next year will have on your nonprofit five years from now. In the fourth column, indicate your collective judgment as to whether you believe your nonprofit should move forward now to grasp each of these opportunities. You will have an opportunity to reconsider these intuitive beliefs after examining some further decision factors in the next worksheet.

WORKSHEET 4.2   **Alternatives for Opportunities for Gain (continued)**

Opportunity	Downside risks and steps the nonprofit can take to counter them	Consequences of NOT pursuing the opportunity	Yes/No
1st Priority			
2nd Priority			
3rd Priority			
4th Priority			
5th Priority			

Earlier, you rated the opportunities quite highly. Therefore, do not be surprised — for now — if you say *Yes* to all five opportunities.

WORKSHEET 4.3   Guidelines for Choosing Alternatives

At this point you have identified and given considerable thought to the threats of accidental loss and opportunities for gains that — for better or worse — may, or may not, surprisingly reshape the future of your nonprofit. You have prioritized all of these threats and opportunities so that you now have five of each that, had you sufficient time and other resources for risk management and everything else, you would agree that all 10 deserve significant management attention within your nonprofit.

But suppose that you do not have enough resources to address them all — that for the next year, starting today, your board has determined that you can deal with only seven of these 10. You may choose any seven of the 10, but only seven. (For simplicity, assume that the costs of dealing with each of the 10 are equal, but that the 10 may differ in the benefits they generate for your nonprofit and for the members of the constituencies your nonprofit serves.) Which seven threats or opportunities will you address right now, and which three do you defer until at least next year?

There is no one correct answer to this question — too much depends on each nonprofit's particular situation. But there are some ways of approaching this question that are better than others. Some guidelines for making strategic risk management decisions that — for your nonprofit, for now — should help you cope with all the uncertainties of intertwined downside and upside risks are:

1. *Be consistent with your collective attitudes toward risk.* If threats of accidental loss worry your leaders more than opportunities for gain attract them, most of the seven projects you select should deal with downside risk.

2. *Serve your nonprofit's mission first.* Putting mission before anything else influences a nonprofit's strategic risk management decisions in two ways. First, to serve its mission, a nonprofit must survive. Ruin in the face of a natural disaster, executive misdeeds, or adverse national economic trends is not an acceptable option. Second, putting mission before money implies that, in making its risk management choices, a nonprofit should not use the same decision criteria that for-profit businesses employ. For a nonprofit, return on investment, probably, is not a valid criterion for deciding what to do; nor are short-term additions to a nonprofit's surplus.

3. *Meet legal requirements.* Everything your nonprofit does must comply with the law and with the terms of the contracts, licenses, and other legal requirements under which it operates. Your strategic risk management actions should do the same. To do otherwise subjects your nonprofit to potential liability.

4. *Respect your nonprofit's culture as you establish strategic risk management priorities.* It is important to follow the cultural practices and norms in your nonprofit so that strategic risk management becomes part of that organizational culture, not something so special and different that it follows *different rules*. For example, if decisions about taking on new projects are generally formulated at the staff level and ratified by the board of directors, it would be foolish for the risk management team to formulate a new initiative in isolation and quickly announce its creation to the staff and board, without first obtaining input.

WORKSHEET 4.3   **Guidelines for Choosing Alternatives (continued)**

Questions:

1. Of the 10 strategic risk management projects in Worksheet 4.2 — five threats of loss and five opportunities for gain — which seven should your nonprofit undertake now?

2. Did you and your colleagues reach this decision readily, or was there much disagreement?

3. Did you agree on the standards for making the choice?

4. If you disagreed, do you agree now, or are the same disagreements likely to arise again when other strategic risk management choices need to be made?

CHAPTER 5

Follow up and Adjust

The underlying purpose of following up and adjusting an organization's past strategic risk management decisions is to see if they were the correct decisions then and if they remain the correct decisions for the future. If they were correct, the organization would have been making progress toward its strategic risk management goals. Furthermore, if the context within which the organization first made those risk management decisions has remained essentially unchanged, then those correct decisions can be reaffirmed. However — and this is the importance of following up and adjusting as the fifth and final step of strategic risk management — if an organization has not been progressing well toward reaching its goals, or if the context of its risk management efforts has changed, then its previous strategic risk management plan must be reviewed and adjusted, perhaps even changed radically. Worksheets 5.1 and 5.2 guide you through this review and possible revision process.

WORSHEET 5.1   Comparing Results With Expectations

Earlier in *The Workbook* you have given much thought to what you expect from strategic risk management. In Worksheet 1.2 (Why You Manage Risk Here) you discussed five basic goals of strategic risk management, and then modified and prioritized them for your particular nonprofit. In Worksheet 4.3 (Guidelines for Choosing Alternatives), you discussed and perhaps modified several standards that all good strategic risk management decisions should meet.

We invite you to summarize your expectations for strategic risk management in the second column of the following chart. In the third column, rate your results — perhaps simply as Good, Average or Poor. Remember that what you are rating is your *progress in moving forward* toward each of your expectations, not whether you have fully met each expectation. The fourth column deals only with possible actions, not firm decisions — as the next worksheet explains, firm decisions should be made only after repeating the entire strategic risk management process.

	EXPECTATIONS	RESULTS	POSSIBLE ACTIONS
Prevent/Pay for Accidental Losses			
Seize Opportunities for Growth			
Serve your Mission			
Meet Legal Requirements			
Reduce Your Uncertainty			
Recognize Your Risk Attitudes			
Be a Good Citizen			
Respect Your Culture			
Stay Within Budget			
Other			
Other			
Other			

Consider completing a chart like this periodically, at least every year or other budgeting or planning period. This will help make strategic risk management an integral part of your overall management process. However, do not let a single year's results alarm you or distract you from long-term trends. Management of either downside or upside risks involves unpredictable events. Substantial fluctuations, for better or worse, are normal. Strategic risk management is an activity that concentrates on trends or factors that will make a difference and that you can manage.

The world always changes. We cannot stop change. We cannot even fully predict change. Therefore, all the factors that influence the decisions your nonprofit makes today about upside and downside risks can change tomorrow — or not. Crucial changes may — or may not — occur, inside or beyond your nonprofit, in the context of your risk management decisions, in the components of the four categories of your key assets, in the downside and upside risks that confront you, in the resources you can devote to risk management, in the cost and availability of the risk management techniques from which you may choose, and in the nature and priority of your nonprofit's risk management goals. Any of these changes may require — and all of these changes together clearly demand — regular renewals of the entire strategic risk management process.

The following chart is a very basic tool that may help you recognize where these changes may occur, assess how these changes may be favorable or unfavorable to your nonprofit's strategic risk management efforts, and consider what changes in your risk management measures might be appropriate if these favorable or unfavorable changes occur. This chart is only a basic tool because a more advanced, complete analysis of possible changes requires detailed knowledge of your nonprofit that only you and your colleagues can bring to the process.

Therefore this chart lists only general categories of the factors that should enter into sound risk management decisions for your nonprofit. For each category, the middle portion of the chart gives you space to note what the favorable and unfavorable changes may be in, say, the next 12 months. In the right column of the chart you can record how your nonprofit might be wise to respond to these changes. Again, the possibilities you put in this column are not firm decisions. Such decisions depend on your renewing the strategic risk management decision cycle.

Factor That May Change	Possible Changes	Reasonable Responses
Context for Risk Management		
Key Assets		
Threats and Opportunities		
Costs/Availability of Risk Management Techniques		
Resources for Managing Risk		
Risk Management Objectives or Decision Criteria		
Other Factors		

Please remember that this chart gives only a very broad overview of possible changes and your nonprofit's possible reasonable responses. A more complete chart could have several hundred rows for more specific changes within the broad categories shown here. Giving some thought to possible changes — for both better and worse — and how you might respond to them broadens your expectations, and makes risk manageable for you and your nonprofit.

Renewing the Process

The core message of *Enlightened Risk Taking* is that nonprofit organizations can more fully accomplish their missions if their leaders accept, and inspire others to implement, a new approach to coping with uncertainty. This new approach recognizes that taking some risks — being prepared for some of the possibilities that the world may be surprisingly different from your expectations — is essential to changing the world in the wondrous ways nonprofits seek. This new approach, strategic risk management, strives to both counter potential losses and seize potential gains to more fully serve each nonprofit's mission.

Having worked with both *Enlightened Risk Taking* and *The Workbook*, you understand the importance of this core message to your nonprofit. You know that strategic risk management is a self-renewing cycle, which is energized by change and by your colleagues who share a desire to accomplish your mission in the face of that change. Your ongoing task is to inspire others within your organization to join you in building an organizational culture that fosters managing risk strategically.

The Epilogue in *Enlightened Risk Taking* offers five steps to inspiring such a culture. Some of these steps you and your colleagues may have already taken, at least tentatively; others will be new to you, and hopefully are in response to these two books. The chart on the next page aims to help you explore the steps you have already taken and those you plan to take soon.

Steps in Building a Risk Management Culture	What You Have Done	What You Will Do
Set up a Body of Customary Beliefs		
Establish, Communicate Your Expectations		
Practice Enlightened Courage to Take Risk		
Teach Others to Talk and Walk Strategic Risk Management		
Consider Benchmarks and Rewards		

The Nonprofit Risk Management Center and its staff recognize that asking you to inspire others to practice strategic risk management is asking you to take some risks yourself. Please do so strategically, countering threats of loss and seizing opportunities for gain, so that your nonprofit will be able to achieve its ambitious goals.

Notes

Notes